ONLINE LEARNING IMPACTS CLASSROOM

DR. RENI FRANCIS

This book has been published with all efforts taken to make the material error-free after the consent of the author. However, the author and the publisher do not assume and hereby disclaim any liability to any party for any loss, damage, or disruption caused by errors or omissions, whether such errors or omissions result from negligence, accident, or any other cause.

While every effort has been made to avoid any mistake or omission, this publication is being sold on the condition and understanding that neither the author nor the publishers or printers would be liable in any manner to any person by reason of any mistake or omission in this publication or for any action taken or omitted to be taken or advice rendered or accepted on the basis of this work. For any defect in printing or binding the publishers will be liable only to replace the defective copy by another copy of this work then available.

To all student teachers pursuing their B.Ed course.

Contents

Acknowledgements

Acknowledgements

"I would maintain that thanks are the highest form of thought, and that gratitude is happiness doubled by wonder." G.K. Chesterton

The hustle bustle in the classroom heard is a vision of the learning in the class. Children with various abilities and capacities work together, learn together for a better tomorrow. The teacher is a role model and always a hope for students to learning and growing.

Even in this phase we see ahead of us, few classroom challenges that hinders learning and growth opportunities. They are few hurdles that need to be addressed and weeds that need to be nipped off at the grassroot level.

It is in this phase we came across this attempt to publish this book on the Action Research conducted in the classroom by the Student Teachers.

We would like to thank Almighty God for giving us the strength in each phase of our life. We would like to thank all the schools for entrusting their support and confidence in conducting this research. My sincere gratitude to all the Student Teachers for their relentless and systematic work carried out during this research.

My gratitude to the Management of Mahatma Education Society's Pillai College of Education and Research, Chembur for their support and motivation for conducting various activities.

We would like to thank our mentors, teachers and all for their continuous guidance and support.

God bless

Thank you.

CHAPTER I

Contents

CHAPTER II

"A study of impact of online learning on academic among the first year B.Ed. students."

Researcher:

Ms. Sudha Gupta

Ms. Sophia D'Souza

Ms. Sushmita Pathak

S.Y.B.Ed (Batch 2020 - 2022), PCER, Chembur.

Guided by: *Dr. Reni Francis, Principal, MES's PCER, Chembur*

ABSTRACT:

Learning may be transferred from a regular face-to-face classroom to a virtual educational setting. Because of its flexibility and accessibility, online learning, which is the newest trend in education, has demonstrated a favourable learning outcome. The influence of online learning on academics was investigated in this study report. A graphical analysis revealed that the majority of students favoured online learning since it offers for more flexibility in operations and easier access to learning materials. It also explains how conventional learning is necessary for an immersive learning environment and how social and physical activities are enhanced. The researcher compiled a list of suggestions for teachers and students to help them feel more confident and fit in with this new trend.

INTRODUCTION THE STUDY

Online learning is getting the education you want, from anywhere in the world, on a schedule that suits your life.

Online learning is when you take courses online instead of in a physical classroom. If your schedule makes it hard to attend classes, if you prefer studying at your own pace or if you live far from campus, online learning might be for you.

With online learning, you can:

- *earn a certificate or diploma without setting foot in a physical classroom*
- *work full-time while you study*
- *set your own schedule: study in the early morning, on your lunch break, or even in the middle of the night*
- *interact with students from across Canada and around the world*
-

get a quality education from the University of Victoria without leaving your home community

Online teaching plays a key role in the education system in India but it became more popular during Covid 19 pandemic because, after March 2020, schools and colleges had been shut down. Online teaching also became an important means of education during the pandemic. Online teaching took place easily and students and teachers didn't need to present together at a particular place.

BACKGROUND OF THE PROBLEM

Online learning is rapidly becoming one of the most effective ways to impart education. The impact of the virus was so strong that online education became a seemingly ubiquitous part of our growing world, which resulted in the closure of schools and no further physical interaction of teachers with students. Fortunately, soon enough most of the schools and educational institutions moved to online mode to resume their studies. As a result, education has changed dramatically, with the distinctive rise of e-learning, whereby teaching is undertaken remotely on digital platforms instead of physical classrooms.

Online classes and technology have emerged as a superhero during the lockdown days. We have all been under house arrest but are still connected with the world of education. Due to the lockdown, students have not been able to stay connected with the outer world and the lack of exposure is evident. The only reprieve for the students' mental well-being has been the transition to online classes. Teachers made sure that the learning for students was not compromised, so they took a great leap forward to find solutions and create new learning environments for their students to ensure that learning never stops. With little time to prepare, curriculums were modified, new lesson plans were created, activities were planned, all so that their students remain actively involved through online learning.

For students, online classes have become an imminent trend in the education sector around the globe. Digital learning has provided easy access to the files and folders that can now be organised and saved without any physical damage. With one click, students can access their notes and assignments without the fear of misplacing or spoiling them. With advanced technology, this mode of learning has not only been simpler but fun and engaging as well. Technology-enabled learning is beneficial and has proven to be more engaging as it helps in making those subjects interactive and fun which are traditionally considered dull by students. It became very convenient for the students to attend classes from anywhere in the world as both classes and learning content was easily accessible at home. Integration of the learning platforms with new-age interactive applications has made online classes more convenient for both students and teachers as more students are able to express their views at the same time using certain online applications. Students have been more particular with their online submission as they are notified on a regular basis and it is an effortless task for the teachers to track down the students who have failed to submit their assignments on time. Online learning has helped students to become independent learners before they make their way into the real world. Students got opportunities to explore new learning applications and platforms during the class, which helped them to develop new skills and capabilities accelerating their growth trajectory. Some of the students have been responding well to the active learning environment created online by the teachers whereas others need a push in fits and starts.

Most of the private and public schools have made a smooth transition to online platforms such as Zoom, Google classrooms, Microsoft teams, etc. while many still find it a herculean task. The challenges of online learning are multifaceted. Online learning has played a crucial role during the pandemic, but its consequences can not be ignored. Online classes can not be accessed by every student due to the unavailability of smartphones, laptops, and network. Unfortunately, the less privileged part of our society has been more on the receiving end of this. This may increase the class and demography-based disparity with respect to access to quality education.

OBJECTIVES OF THE STUDY

1. *To study the impact of online learning.*

2. *To study the impact of academic in online learning.*

3.

To suggest measure for enhancing online learning.

STATEMENT OF PROBLEM

" A study on Impact of online learning on academic among the students of F.Y. B.Ed."

Conceptual definition of the problem:

Study:

Conceptual meaning: *The devotion of time and attention to gain knowledge of an academic*

subject, especially by means of books.

Operational definition: *To find the Impact of online learning on academic among the students*

Online learning:

Conceptual definition: *Online learning is education that takes place over the Internet. It is often referred to as "e- learning" among other terms.*

Operational definition: *To adapt and learn about the effects of online learning on students' academics. Online blended learning has been shown to be more flexible and facilitates quick access to learning materials.*

Sustainable development goals:

Conceptual definition: *The Sustainable Development Goals are the blueprint to achieve a better and more sustainable future for all. They address the global challenges we face, including poverty, inequality, climate change, environmental degradation, peace, and justice.*

F.Y. B.Ed. students:

Conceptual definition: *Students studying in F.Y, B.Ed. from PCER College, Chembur.*

Operational definition: *Students studying in F.Y, B.Ed. from PCER College, Chembur.*

Delimitation of the study

The study is delimited to;

The students of PCER College, Chembur.

Students of F.Y. B.Ed. only.

Students studying in English Medium School.

METHODOLOGY OF THE STUDY

The study was survey time method. Google form was based on the topic ***Impact of online learning on Academic.*** *There were 15 statements made in the google form. It had 5 options. The researcher has made the google form based on* ***Impact of online learning on Academic*** *topic of research.*

SAMPLE

The sample size is a term used in market research for defining the number of subjects included in a sample size. By sample size, we understand a group of subjects that are selected from the general population and is considered a representative of the real population for that specific study. This number is usually represented by n. The size of a sample influences two statistical properties: 1) the precision of our estimates and 2) the power of the study to draw conclusions

For example, if we want to predict how the population in a specific age group will react to a new product, we can first test it on a sample size that is representative of the targeted population. The sample size, in this case, will be given by the number of people in that age group that will be surveyed.

The sample for the study is 15 number of students of first year B.Ed. students from MES Pillai College of Education and Research,

Chembur- Mumbai.

RESEARCH TOOLS AND TECHNIQUES

The researcher made google form with 15 number of statements with 5 options of answers based on the topic ***Impact of online learning on Academic.*** *The google form was first made by the researcher. This was then presented to the research guide to suggestion and modification. After the research guide the final tool questions were prepared as a google form.*

The google form consist of preliminary information of the google form.

SELECTION OF THE TOOL

The tools used in this study is Questionnaire. The researcher made google form consisting of 15 statements each having four options as answers based on the topic 'Impact of Online learning on social skills.

PREPARATION OF TOOLS

The Google form was first made by the researcher. This was then presented to the research guide for suggestions and modifications. After the discussion with the research guide, the final tool consisting of 15 statements was prepared as a Google form. The Google form consisted of preliminary information of a student's respondent.

The questionnaire tool consisted of 15 statements in which the students had to choose 1 from the given 5 options. The students had to tick on the option which they felt was most suited to them. These statements were simply framed so that the students could easily understand and tick on the option which suited them.

ANALYSIS OF DATA:

Although many groups, organizations, and experts have different ways to approach data analysis, most of them can be distilled into a one-size-fits-all definition. Data analysis is the process of cleaning, changing, and processing raw data, and extracting actionable, relevant information that helps businesses make informed decisions. The procedure helps reduce the risks inherent in decision-making by providing useful insights and statistics, often presented in charts, images, tables, and graphs.

It's not uncommon to hear the term "big data" brought up in discussions about data analysis. Data analysis plays a crucial role in processing big data into useful information.

1. *Online blended learning has impacted your learning habits*

Explanation:

The maximum responses received for the above statement is sometimes which is 57.1%. Online learning isn't the easiest transition. Not only does it take a change in learning style, but ***it takes a drastic change in study habits****. For a lot of students, online learning requires more self-discipline, a more organized schedule, and more self-motivation.*

1. *Online learning causes barriers between the learning style and academic achievements.*

Explanation: *learning styles are widely accepted in education as a way to promote the idea that every student learns differently. The option selected for the above statement is sometimes by 64.3 % of candidates as the learner may be at their own space to learn during the online learning which makes the learner comfortable and learn better.*

3. Online learning provides theoretical and practical experience.

Explanation: *Practical knowledge is knowledge that is acquired by day-to-day hands-on experiences. In other words, practical knowledge is gained through doing things; it is very much based on real-life endeavors and tasks. 50% of the participant have selected 'sometimes' as during the online learning practical experience and learning is not always possible as compared to physical classes.*

4. *The use of communication technology in e-learning enhances the academic achievement of students.*

Explanation: *The study found out that e-learning encourages self-learning, and gives a feeling of comfort in use and interaction promoting greater flexibility in learning time, in addition to motivating the students and enhancing their academic performance. There are varied replies received the above statements. Hence 35% of the participants have selected sometimes.*

5. *Online learning acts as a versatile platform for teaching and learning.*

Explanation: *The 50% of participants have chosen sometimes for the above statement.*

Online learning has made learning material easily accessible. Children and teachers can check out learning material and many abroad speakers can share their knowledge through online platforms. But such accessibility is sometimes not possible in the rural areas due to lack of technological uses and appliances.

6.

Spending long time in online learning makes the student lose their interest in the activities.

Explanation: *43.8% of the participants have chosen 'sometimes' for the above statement as E-Learning can cause social Isolation. E-Learning requires strong self-motivation and time management skills. Lack of communicational skill development in online students. Cheating prevention during online assessments is complicated.*

7.

Less interaction due to no contact between teacher's students makes the learning more boring and easily lose concentration.

Explanation: *37.5 % of the students have selected 'sometimes' for the above statement. As the statements says there is less interaction* *between the students and the teachers makes learning more boring as the students are on the other side of the screen and it becomes difficult for the teachers to get some children participate in online activities.*

8. *Changes in learning habits have hampered the students grasping skills during the online learning.*

Explanation:*44.4 % of the students have selected 'sometimes' for the above statement. There are number of technologies available for online education but sometimes they create a lot of difficulties. These difficulties and problems associated with modern technology range from downloading errors, issues with installation, login problems, problems with audio and video, and so on.*

9.

Online quizzes, games and assignments makes learning engaging and interesting.

Explanation: *The maximum up to 44.4% replies are received as 'Always' on the above statement. Teachers have to prepare a variety of methods and techniques to teach a subject that is effective during e-learning. The use of slideshow, videos, pictures, games, and online generator to create quizzes are things that teachers can use to support the teaching.*

10.

Online blended learning makes practical teaching difficult.

Explanation: *For the above statement maximum of the participate has selected sometimes and frequently i.e 33.3% equally. Practical teaching leads to more of hands on learning and experiential learning which is difficult during the online learning.*

11.

Lack of mobile gadgets to use for online classes hampers a students education.

Explanation:

The answer for the above question was chosen by pupils 27.8% sometimes, 33.3% always, 22.2% frequently, 11.1% rarely and 8% never. The results may be basically based on the rural areas where there is lack of technology and also considering financially weak families who can not afford the gadgets for their online learning.

12.

Online learning offers students the accessibility of time and place in education.

Explanation

The answer for the above question was chosen 11.11% frequently, 50% always, 33.3%sometimes and 5% rarely. Online courses provide greater flexibility, allowing students to do their work when they are most capable of it, rather than when the class is scheduled. They are easier to access for students with mobility issues, who can work from their homes instead of trying to navigate inaccessible campuses and classrooms.

13.

Online learning causes social isolation and results causing barrier in learning process

Explanation:

The answer for the above question was chosen 44.4%sometimes, 16.7% never, 22.2%,rarely,8% frequently and 11.1%always. As a result, many of the students and teachers who inevitably spend much of their time online can start experiencing signs of social isolation, due to the ***lack of human communication in their lives***

14\.

Online education allows student to learn and access the learning material across the nation.

Explanation:

The answer for the above question was chosen 33.33% frequently, 33.3% always, 33.3%sometimes..Distance learning when learning on-demand via a wonderfully designed syllabus with videos for whenever consumption and assignments to be done at convenience.

15.

Online learning causes lack of effective communication where students have the sense of loneliness affecting the academic performance.

Explanation:

The answer for the above question was chosen by pupils 22.2% never, 16.7%frequently,27.8%always,33.3% sometimes. To summarize, the study aimed to explore whether online learning has an effect on communication between instructors and students in a negative way, if online learning affects students' productivity levels. As well as, to evaluate and suggest ways of improving effective communication between instructors and students in online courses.

SUGGESTIONS FOR STUDENTS

1. ***Establish a productive learning environment***

Working on assignments from a slouched position and streaming Netflix at the same time is not ideal if you aim to be productive. Dr. Hatten, who specializes in online teaching and learning, recommends that students choose an area in their homes that's free from common distractions.

2. ***Set a schedule for completing and reviewing assignments***

Working on three courses at the same time can cause for an individual to experience a high level of stress, but this can be avoided if you allocate specific times to work on each class. One example Dr. Hatten shared is working on one class between the hours of 11 a.m. to 3 p.m. This schedule allows students to create a type of structure often seen with traditional, in-person classes.

3. ***Seek virtual interactions with your peers***

Studying with a group of peers in the library or simply receiving on-the-spot clarifications from classmates is obviously not possible during this time. However, forming virtual interactions through platforms such as GroupMe or Microsoft Teams is a feasible action you could take in order to maintain that sense of collaboration and community.

4. ***Use the 'chunking' strategy to section out tasks***

The term "chunking" refers to taking a large task or a large amount of information and dividing it into smaller units. Instead of staring at a computer screen for three hours at a time, Dr. Hatten suggests that students "chunk" their time by following a specific pattern.

5. ***Try to increase your interest in the work***

There may be times where you go over an assignment or task that seems rather tedious. Instead of waving it off as the days go by, think about how you can turn the assignment or task into an engaging one. Using this strategy means using your imagination to creatively modify the work you'll turn in.

6. *Make the work you're doing online more personally significant*

You may experience a lack of motivation when you feel unconnected to an assignment or task being given. Dr. Park encourages students who are confronted by this feeling to think critically about how that assignment could be useful in helping them in the future.

SUGGESTIONS FOR TEACHERS

1. *Utilize a variety of technology options.*

Teachers should plan to spend the first several days of class helping students understand the technology and learn how to work with it. Practice exercises are a great way for students to try out the technology and make sure they understand what to do, asking questions and getting help before projects begin. This learning curve time and hands-on practice will help students and those who are teaching them alike be prepared and work out any kinks in the system.

2. Connect to students individually.

While those who teach need to create good strategies that will help them work with all of their students, when they are in an online environment it is extremely important to also meet with students individually. In traditional classroom settings where those teaching can see how students are doing daily, interact with them one-on-one if they have questions, and speak to them in private if needed. Teaching online can still allow for those same opportunities for students. It can happen as teachers open hours and virtual resources for students to log on and chat or message them if they have questions or concerns, or teachers can video call and check in with students every week or two in order to make sure they are doing well. These meetings can help teachers assess how students are doing academically with the online courses and lessons, as well as socially and mentally. Good education involves students who are successful in other areas of their life, and teachers play an important role in this wellness. Meeting one-on-one with students will help teachers evaluate how their students are doing.

3. Prepare to work with parents.

As teachers spend less or no time with their students in an actual classroom, parental involvement will play a huge role in their school success. It's extremely valuable to teachers to communicate with parents about how they anticipate the school year will go so parents can help ensure students have the equipment, setup, and technological skills they'll need to succeed. Parents will also be needed to help answer questions and work on assignments for the online courses and lessons, so it's vital for teachers to communicate regularly with them about what the expectations for their students are. Now more than ever, parents are playing an integral role in their child's virtual education as it is happening at home, with them nearby. Instead of teacher's being able to answer a question or help fix a problem, parents will be needed. Working with parents and talking to them often can help them feel successful as they help their learner navigate the school year.

4. Consider new learning methods.

There are a wide variety of learning styles that students have, and a wide variety of learning methods that teachers can utilize in the classroom to help their learners. As teachers are transitioning to online learning, it may be a good time to evaluate their lesson plans and tactics and decide if they are the best approach for students. For example, many teachers may opt to do a flipped classroom style. This teaching method involves learners viewing video lectures and instruction as homework after school, and then during class time when they are online with the teacher, they go over problems and do assignments. This allows them to watch videos and learn concepts in the afternoon and, and spend the school day asking their teacher questions and solidifying their understanding. This learning model is a great option for digital learning, as it gives students the opportunity to interact with their teacher and ask questions for the majority of their school day. Similarly an inquiry based learning model where teachers act more as a facilitator for learning instead of the authoritative figure can be great for online classes.

5. ***Provide collaboration and socialization opportunities.***

School isn't just about education, important social skills are developed in the classroom as well. Teachers can continue to foster socialization and collaboration even in their online classroom. Teachers can create group projects and have online students meet on Google Hangouts or Zoom to connect and work together. Teachers can also hold smaller group sessions to work with students, allowing them to chat more openly and work together in a more conducive environment. Some teachers may opt to start their school day with a chance to visit, have students take time each day sharing about what they have been doing, or even have a way for students to share jokes or funny stories. Chat channels can allow students to discuss things with their online class and have easy ways to connect even when they are far apart. Teachers can allow "recess" or a break that lets students just visit, laugh, and have socializing opportunities. This kind of socialization is important to a happy, exciting classroom for students. Building these relationships among their peers and with you as the teacher is critical for a positive experience.

Conclusion

Online education is known to offer the benefit of synergy. Here, the format employed makes room for dynamic communications between students and the teachers. Through these communications, sources are shared, and an open-ended synergy evolves through a learning process. When each person bestows a view or opinion through discussions and comments on others' work course, it benefits the student to learn better. This unique advantage is manifested in a student-centred virtual learning environment that online learning format alone can contribute.

With online classes, we don't need to travel to a different city or commute long distances. We can stay where we are and keep our current job while we work toward improving our career with an online degree. Online education also helps digital nomads—someone who espouses a technology-enabled or location-independent lifestyle. We can watch lectures and complete our coursework wherever we are.

Whether we are a full-time or part-time online student, the online education experience provides a much more manageable schedule. Online education has gained much approval on account of its cheapness. Such is the fact that online courses are more affordable than those offered at schools or colleges. While studying in universities, we may have to spend some money such as transportation, lodging, and meals, online education may not require such expenses.

One of the important aspects of online learning is its inherent flexibility, however, there is a catch, one has to be extremely self-motivated. The best online students develop various approaches for staying up to date on their coursework. Things like setting aside time every week to study and create a workspace with minimal distractions can help immensely.

Online education's potential advantages involve increased educational access; it provides a high-quality learning opportunity, improves student outcomes and skills, and expands educational choice options. Therefore, location, time, and quality are no longer considered factors in seeking degree courses or higher education because of online education.

REFERENCES

- https://www.aplustopper.com/essay-on-online-education/
- https://www.oecd.org/coronavirus/policy-responses/strengthening-online-learning
- https://eric.ed.gov/?q=Academic+online+learning+
- https://www.mdpi.com/2227-7102/11/11/715/htm

- https://pesquisa.bvsalud.org/global-literature-on-novel-coronavirus-2019-ncov/resource/pt/covidwho-1512186
- https://eric.ed.gov/?id=EJ1322863
- https://scholar.google.co.in/scholar?q=The+Impact+of+Content+Co-Creation+on+Academic+Achievement
- https://ncert.nic.in/division/der/pdf/ERIC_Guidelines.pdf

CHAPTER III

"A study of impact of online learning on technological adaptability among B.Ed students"

Researcher: Ms. Vaishnavi Perumal

S.Y.B.Ed (Batch of 2020-2022), PCER, Chembur

Guided by: Dr. Reni Francis, Principal, MES's PCER, Chembur

Abstract: *Although many people still consider traditional classes as the best way for learning but in this technological age online classes system of learning proves to be a great alternative of traditional classes. In this research paper, the researcher studied the impact of online learning on technological adaptability among B.Ed students. The aim of this study was to verify if technological factors have an influence on persistence in online courses. The study was a survey type method. Google form was used for the survey. There were 15 statements made for the google form.*

The statements were marked based on Never, Rarely , Sometimes, Always. The sample of the study is 16 number of students of First year B.Ed of Mahatma Education Society Pillai college of Education and Research, Chembur

Keywords: *Technological adaptability, online learning*

Introduction to the study

In the 21st century, technology is becoming an essential to our everyday life. Even kids these days as young as three to four years old knows how to use an ipad or an iphone. So society has made use of the technology we have today for learning. It has moved on from the traditional classroom and whiteboard style to online learning with the supplementation of the mobile phone. There are various benefits of online and mobile learning however there are benefits that the traditional method of learning that technology cannot overcome. Online learning is the process of studying without having to physically attending classes or lectures and mobile learning is to help online learning more efficient by quickly being able to obtain information via the internet through the smart phones we have today. By not having to physically attend lectures, students are able to do their assignments anywhere. Technology has impacted every aspect of life and education is no exception . The education process has evolved as more people make use of technological devices and so education no longer starts or ends in the classroom. Technology in education is like a double edged sword, you can either use it to your advantage or to your disadvantage.

Although many people still consider traditional classes as the best way for learning but in this technological age online classes system of learning proves to be a great alternative of traditional classes. In online class system students have the chance to study from the easy of their home. Students can take classes at the time when they preferred as most of the classes are recorded. Online classes system of learning helps participants to learn whenever they want to learn, leaving them the freedom to choose the time for study. Many schools, institutions and universities are providing online classes free of costs. Thus online classes are helpful for those students who earlier could not pay fees. Now they are accessing these online classes online for free. Among the advantages of online classes system of learning there are the responsibility and self-discipline of students in online class system.

At school or in traditional class system students learn how to make friends, how to behave with teacher and friends, how to get rid of disappointment etc. The main work of personality development of students can be done through traditional classes. In online classes these all are missing. Online learning cannot offer face to face human interaction which are very important for personality development.

Online classes system can be difficult for some persons who don't know the proper use of technological instruments. For small children online classes requires great disciplines and practice. It also requires more interventions of parents in case of small children. In online classes student use electronic devices like mobile, tablet, laptops or computer. Use of these

devices for longer time will badly affect the health of students..

BACKGROUND OF THE PROBLEM

The term "online learning" is defined as a use of the Internet to deliver instructional content to students, either for education or training purposes. It is often abbreviated as e learning .Online learning facilitates access to information, courses, systems and services worldwide through relatively inexpensive computer networks

Online learning is rapidly becoming one of the most effective ways to impart education. The COVID-19 pandemic has become a global health issue and has had a major impact on education. Consequently, half way through the second semester of the academic year 2019/ 2020, learning methods were delivered through distance learning (DL) . The impact of the virus was so strong that online education became a seemingly ubiquitous part of our growing world, which resulted in the closure of schools and no further physical interaction of teachers with students. Fortunately, soon enough most of the schools and educational institutions moved to online mode to resume their studies. As a result, education has changed dramatically, with the distinctive rise of e-learning, whereby teaching is undertaken remotely on digital platforms instead of physical classrooms. For students, online classes have become an imminent trend in the education sector around the globe. Digital learning has provided easy access to the files and folders that can now be organised and saved without any physical damage. With one click, students can access their notes and assignments without the fear of misplacing or spoiling them. With advanced technology, this mode of learning has not only been simpler but fun and engaging as well. Technology-enabled learning is beneficial and has proven to be more engaging as it helps in making those subjects interactive and fun which are traditionally considered dull by students. It became very convenient for the students to attend classes from anywhere in the world as both classes and learning content was easily accessible at home. Integration of the learning platforms with new-

age interactive applications has made online classes more convenient for both students and teachers as more students are able to express their views at the same time using certain online applications. Students have been more particular with their online submission as they are notified on a regular basis and it is an effortless task for

the teachers to track down the students who have failed to submit their assignments on time. Online learning has helped students to become independent learners before they make their way into the real world. Students got opportunities to explore new learning applications and platforms during the class, which helped them to develop new skills and capabilities accelerating their growth trajectory. Some of the students have been responding well to the active learning environment created online by the teachers whereas others need a push in fits and starts.

Most of the private and public schools have made a smooth transition to online platforms such as Zoom, Google classrooms, Microsoft teams, etc. while many still find it a herculean task. The challenges of online learning are multifaceted. Online learning has played a crucial role during the pandemic, but its consequences can not be ignored. Online classes can not be accessed by every student due to the unavailability of smartphones, laptops, and network. Unfortunately, the less privileged part of our society has been more on the receiving end of this. This may increase the class and demography-based disparity with respect to access to quality education.

Moreover, lecturers have a significant impact on student learning and are responsible for bringing technology-based learning (Mardiana, 2018). Technological changes in education have created new ways to learn and learn. Students and lecturers bring their computers to study. Hence, lecturers must adopt a unique teaching methodology, and students follow a new style of learning. Changes in technology enable lecturers to access information on a global scale through the Internet to improve their learning, and students use Internet resources to enrich learning experiences (Banks, 2017). University should take the actions (technology policy, lecturer recruitment plan, and faculty restructuring). It means that change must start from class to class, with each lecturer personally adjusting the way they learn. So it requires efforts to become part of the lecturers because they must educate in new skills before continuing the learning knowledge (Boyd, 2014). In reality, many lecturers in Indonesia cannot adopt the latest technology of teaching. In pandemic

Covid 19, the learning process is mostly online learning. The unpreparedness of lecturers in teaching online makes the learning chaotic (Lederman, 2020). On the other side, the efforts to advance education using technology have been conveyed by Indonesia Ministry Nadiem Makarim, which stated that the use of technology is a necessity in school, but the contribution of educational technology platforms to the education system is still declared inadequate (Soegiono, 2019). As the interview with some students, they protest because learning did not work correctly. Some many tasks and quizzes do not need to give to students to make student work pile up and not complete. Lecturers give online learning the same as providing knowledge in the classroom, even though the assignment should give in phased online learning. Students spend a lot of money doing tasks resulting in learning costs charged to students (Adit, 2020); (Matas & Cameron, 2005). What needs in teaching by using technology is to have the right targets or by using teaching and learning methodologies that tailors and affordable, impressive (Hayes, 2017)? In the previous research by Howard & Mozejko (2015) stated that institutional policies, curriculum, and changes in digital technology in the classroom make lecturers have to change the way they teach. In assigning tasks must be following the online curriculum of the institution or campus. Lecturers involved in online learning must demonstrate learning that is different from in the classroom. Another research by Ertmer & Otenbreit-Leftwich (2010) stated that assist lecturers in online teaching, an institution or campus must facilitate meaningful learning that enables students to build deeper and connected knowledge that applies to real situations. Therefore, online teaching can work well by adopting new approaches in teaching and changing the content or context of learning. Groff (2013) mentioned that apart

from being a resource, technology can play a role as the primary key holder in the learning element. The power to change teaching by introducing a new model that connects lecturers and students with content, resources, and professional systems that enhance their teaching

(Hamiti & Reka, 2012). Based on the researchers above, this research concluded that lecturers" adaptability in technological change is a process that includes the ability and skills in the use of technology that has an open-source on the Internet that can share learning content and involve institutions or campuses and students

I believe that learning never stopped, in fact, it evolved itself not just to survive but to thrive and technology has proven to be the most important enabler of the same which in itself is an invention that is an outcome of learning. Technology has helped in learning and learning has led to the advancement of technology. Students need both parents" and teachers" guidance as they navigate through this difficult time to learn more and more. Both offline learning and e-learning would go hand-in-hand and online education will eventually become an integral component of school education. Somewhere in the future, education is going to be hybrid. During Covid, technology has become a part of academics and is here to stay. Online applications and programs have helped both teachers and students to develop new skills and capabilities that supported them and enhance their knowledge. Online teaching can not replace the position of traditional classroom teaching and we will need to get back to traditional teaching after the pandemic ends.

OBJECTIVES OF THE STUDY

To study the impact of online learning

To study the impact of technological adaptability in online learning

To suggest measures for enhancing online learning

STATEMENT OF PROBLEM

"A study of impact of online learning on technological adaptability among B.Ed students."

Conceptual definition of the Problem:

Study:

Conceptual meaning: The devotion of time and attention to gain knowledge of an academic subject, especially by means of books.

Operational definition: To find the awareness about of impact of online learning on technological adaptability among students.

Online learning :

Conceptual definition: the instructional method of delivering course content remotely outside the physical classroom through the Internet and other digital technologies

Operational definition: A learning system based on formalised teaching but with the help of electronic resources is known as E-learning. While teaching can be based in or out of the classrooms, the use of computers and the Internet forms the major component of E learning..

Technological adaptability :

Conceptual definition: The fact that the originally intended use of a technology or service

is sometimes changed or adapted by people or organizations in practice. Technological adaptability is the firm's strength in obtaining and utilizing the technological resources and systems as per the prevailing market conditions

F.Y.B.Ed students:

Conceptual definition: Students studying in Class F.Y.B.Ed of MES Pillai College of Education and Research

Operational definition: Students studying in Class F.Y.B.Ed of MES Pillai College of Education and Research

Delimitation of the study

The study was limited to First year students of Mahatma Education Society Pillai College, Chembur

Methodology of the study

The study was a survey type method. Google form was used for the survey. Google form was made on the topic A study of impact of online learning on technological adaptability on B.Ed students. There were 15 statements made for the google form. The statements were marked based on Never, Rarely , Sometimes, Always . The researcher has made the google form based on the topic of research.

Sample of the study

The sample size was 16. The sampling technique used was purposive as the students were from class F.Y.B.Ed of Mahatma Education Society Pillai College, Chembur was taken for the study.

Tool used to collect data

The researcher made a google form consisting of 15 number of statements with 4 options of answers based on the topic „ A study of impact of online learning on technological adaptability. The google form was first made by the researcher . This was then presented to the research guide for suggestions and modifications. After the discussion with research guide, the final tool consisting of 15 questions was prepared as a google form. The google form consisted of preliminary information of the student respondents.

Analysis of Data

For the research, the google form was sent to the entire class of class F.Y.B.Ed of Mahatma Education Society Pillai College, Chembur. Thus, data was collected by mailing a google form that consisted 15 questions in all. Out of which 4 were multiple choice question with 4 options. Another 4 questions were with two choice of yes/no for the respondent to choose. The response from 16 students was received. The data received from these 16 students was analysed. The responses have been gathered, studied and pie charts/graphs have been generated for better understanding and have helped to draw conclusions for the action research.

In order to find out about the student's understanding of Technological adaptability , the following questions asked were:

1. In online learning, getting adapted to new technologies by students directly affects the students effectiveness of online learning

Interpretation:

25% strongly agree. Almost 44% people have agreed to this statement. 31.3% are neutral No one has disagreed / strongly disagreed to this statement which shows people are either neutral or agree with this..

2. There is no significant difference in the student perception towards latest technology across the age

Interpretation:

43.8 % disagree to this statement. (a small portion also strongly disagrees). Percentage of people who agree towards this statement is equal to the number of people who are neutral towards this statement

Maximum respondents disagree with this statement, which clearly shows people believe that there is significant difference in student perception towards latest technology across the age.

3.Did you face any problem while getting adapted to new technologies

Interpretation:

Almost 81 % say they did not face any problem getting adapted to new technologies. People saying this implies students are more comfortable with digital World.

4.In online learning, adaptation of new technologies enable students to deepen their understanding of difficult concepts

Interpretation:

50% respondents agree with this statement. 25% are neutral and a very small part of respondents disagree with this statement . Respondents feel that online learning using new technologies can make

difficult concepts simpler.

5. Technological adaptation provides students with easy to access information, accelerated learning and fun opportunities

Interpretation:

Almost 56% of the respondents agree , 31 % strongly agree, others are neutral. No one disagrees with the statement. People are either neutral or agree with this statement completely, which clearly means Technological adaptation is a fun way of learning

6. Has technological adaptations helped keep engagement in virtual classrooms high? Interpretation:

The number for strongly agree, agree, neutral is more or less the same. Technological adaptation has definitely kept classroom engagement high due to various interesting factors.

7. Technological adaptations in online learning has opposed to the past tradition of one sided conversation

Interpretation:

44% which is almost half of the crowd being neutral. Very few respondents strongly disagree with the statement. So we can conclude that people don "t strongly believe that technological adaptation in online learning has opposed to the past tradition of one sided conversation

8. With Technical adaptations learning is becoming more feasible day by day.

Interpretation:

Majority of the crowd agrees with this statement. Online learning has definitely made life more easy due to its flexibility

9. We must have the knowledge of basic technologies to handle the forth coming or advanced adaptations in technology

Interpretation:

Almost 88% of the respondents say that its necessary to have basic knowledge of technologies to handle the advanced work. Its clear that for a person to go ahead with new technology its important to have basic knowledge about the same..

10.Can each and every student in the classroom easily adapt to the technology changes during online learning.

Interpretation: Although there are quite mixed opinions for this statement, a very few people strongly disagree that every student can easily adapt to technology Finally, it differs from student to student as how much is he/she able to adapt to new technologies

11. My ability to retain information has reduced due to online learning.

Interpretation: The number of people who agree with this statement is equal to the people who disagree with this.

It again differs from person to person whether he /she has faced problems in retaining information

12. Over dependence on technology has led to students losing their creativity, ability to think.

Interpretation:

Although there are quite mixed opinions for this statement, a very few people strongly disagree that over dependence on technology had led to lose of students creativity and ability to think

This is moreover a neutral statement and depends on the person involved.

13. Every school is capable of adopting new technological products

Interpretation: People have mixed opinions with this statement and it depends on school if they have the capability to adopt new technological products. Every school may not be capable of adopting new technological products

14. Maintaining ethics during online lectures and online exams have reduced. Interpretation:

Almost half of the respondents feel maintaining ethics during online classes have reduced. People may have lost ethics during online class due to flexibility of sitting at home, also because they may not have to answer teachers face to face and can escape abruptly.

15. Adopting new technological products will make it easier for future educators to assess students

Interpretation:

Almost half of the respondents strongly agree that adopting new technologies can definitely make life easier in future. Its important to get adapted to new technologies for professional growth as well as to make life easier.

Findings:

After analysing the results, it was concluded that the students liked the online classes but are not interested in continuing the same way after the lockdown.

They felt that classroom teaching was more effective than online learning due to issues related to topic understanding, net connectivity, and lack of practical and/or demonstrations. Hence, certain improvements must be made to increase its acceptability amongst students.

Suggestions for Teachers/ Educational Institutions

Online learning can be enhanced by giving learners control of their interactions with media and prompting learner reflection

Provide devices for students to work if at all possible or at least ensure that any online learning activities can be completed with a smartphone

Institutions that offer online courses or programs should make an effort to present to faculty the research about the efficacy of fully online and blended learning for achieving student learning outcomes

Institutions that offer online courses or programs should develop reward systems that encourage innovation in teaching.

Information security training should be customized to the audience

Researchers studying online teaching and learning should prioritize collecting data about the efficacy of tools, technologies, and practices for which the evidence base is not yet robust

Teachers must ensure that students participate in the course's online forum to help better understand course materials and engage with fellow classmates

Suggestions for Student

Regardless of where you choose to work, consider turning your cell phone off to avoid losing focus every time a text message or notification pops up. And if you're still having trouble resisting the temptation to check your email or surf the web, try downloading a website blocker.

- *Make use of online tools*
- *Improve your digital literacy*
- *Stay positive and informed*
- *Ask for help*

Conclusion

Recent years have yielded significant advances in computing and communication technologies, with profound impacts on society. Technology is transforming the way we work, play, and interact with others. From these technological capabilities, new industries, organizational forms, and business models are emerging. Technological advances can create enormous economic and other benefits, but can also lead to significant changes for workers. After analysing the results, it was concluded that the students liked the online classes but are not interested in continuing the same way after the lockdown. They felt that classroom teaching was more effective than online learning due to issues related to topic understanding, net connectivity, and lack of practical and/or demonstrations. Hence, certain improvements must be made to increase its acceptability amongst students.

References

- https://www.researchgate.net/publication/299533794_

- https://www.educause.edu/ecar/research-publications
- https://www.techlearning.com/tl-advisor-blog/8
- https://ccrc.tc.columbia.edu/media/k2/attachments/adaptability-to-online-learning
- https://kiron.ngo/community/adapting-to-online-learning
- https://link.springer.com/article/10.1007/s10639-021-10507-1
- https://www.tandfonline.com/doi/full/10.1080/03323315.2021.1916559

CHAPTER IV

"Impact Of Online Learning On Digital Hygiene

Researcher:

Ms. Yogita Pervi

Ms. Shalki

S.Y.B.Ed (Batch of 2021-2022), PCER, Chembur

Guided by: Dr. Reni Francis, Principal, MES's PCER, Chembur

Abstract: *Generally, it has been seen that students are aware about the cyber security about some are new to the term digital hygiene. In this research paper, the researcher studied the awareness of "The Study of impact of online learning on Digital hygiene. F.Y.BE.d.*

It was found through a graphical data The students were aware that antivirus is one of the practices that will help the system working in proper way. Also it was found that some of them are not sure for the answers related to malware. As malware comes in so many variants, there are numerous methods to infect computer systems. For example, Virus, a malware program that when executed, replicates by inserting copies of itself into other computer programs, data files, or firmware, here 11% of students were not sure about the properties of malware.

The concept related to remote learning was also cleared by this analysis. For remote learning mostly apps are used by the learners and sometimes without knowing the features of the apps there are chances that the system might get caught of any malware. Around 64% of students response seems to be not sure about the use of apps are safe or not. Likewise using personal hotspot is always a safer option; the analysis showed around 35% of students is not sure or not aware. From the data collected it can be seen that 47% - 52% students has a very good opinion for separating personal and work stuff and avoid using personal emails for work applications. This shows that students are very much aware of their personal and work life and knows how to maintain the balance between work and personal life.

Introduction to the study

Online learning is education that takes place over the Internet. It is often referred to as "e-learning" among other terms. However, online learning is just one type of "distance learning" – the umbrella term for any learning that takes place across distance and not in a traditional classroom.This type of learning is a form of education over the internet and in a remote setting. You get to indulge in an education method in an entirely virtual environment.

Even though its adoption was rapid during the pandemic, this learning method predates the virus.

It was first introduced when the internet came into existence. Online education was a distance learning method amongst higher education students. Today, it enables students to learn, irrespective of geography. You could engage with any institution or look for academic e-learning opportunities. Indeed, online learning is a way for students to learn at their own pace and flexibility. This internet-based learning environment connects diverse backgrounds and brings together different perspectives.

Online learning is the newest and most popular form of Distance education today. Within the past decade it has Had a major impact on postsecondary education and the Trend is only increasing. In this workshop we will explore what the experience of Online learning is like for students and how it has Changed the role of the instructor. Online learning is education that takes place over the Internet. It is often referred to as "e-Learning" among other terms. However, online learning is just one type of "distance learning" – The umbrella term for any learning that takes place across distance and not in a traditional Classroom

From this simple definition comes an almost in finite number of ways to teach and learn outside of traditional classrooms and away from college campuses. With online education, students can turn anywhere with Internet access and electricity into a classroom. It can include audio, video, text, animations, virtual training environments and live chats with professors. It's a rich learning environment with much more flexibility than a traditional classroom. When used to its full potential, online education has been shown to be more effective than pure face-to-face instruction. It can be engaging, fun and tailored to almost anyone's schedule.

Digital hygiene encourages individuals to perform routine-based digital practices in order to minimize cyber risks. In contrast to cyber security's use of military or war-like metaphors, the narrative of digital hygiene returns to illness as metaphor, as introduced by Susan Sontag in a 1977 lecture, which provided the basis for her famous short book Illness as Metaphor (1978).

The use of metaphors to explain and guide concepts, in both everyday vernacular and authoritative rhetorics, has the tendency to instill morality that carries a disciplinary power. Back in 2014, the Institute of Network Culture's (INC) Theory On Demand publication already provided insight into how we can consider 'digital hygiene' as a metaphor. In a text titled Transcoding the Digital, the late Marianne van den Boomen unravels 'digital praxis', a coherent set of everyday practices that involve the manipulation, modification, and construction of digital-symbolical objects that "somehow matter socially".

Background of the Problem

During my internship I learnt my new things that can be done with the help of online learning resources. Due to pandemic everything went online in almost every field, teaching is also one of them. I felt that online resources are helpful but there are some important facts that need to be taken care of. Like there were new IDs were made with passwords to use certain resources, so it was important that you have to remember the passwords and do not forget them. Use of social media was increased during this time so there was chance of identity thefts. Updating the software systems of computers or laptops became important, protecting from malware, using antivirus etc. all these factors came into the concept of impact of online learning.

Objectives of the Study

- *To study the impact of online learning.*
- *To study the impact of digital hygiene in online learning.*
- *To suggest measures for enhancing online learning.*

Statement of Problem

"The Study Of Impact Of Online Learning On Digital Hygiene" among F.Y.BE.d students.

Conceptual definition of the Problem:

Study:

Digital hygiene is the catch-all term for the practices and behaviours related to cleaning up and maintaining your digital world. You might hear this being called cyber hygiene or internet hygiene—these all really mean the same thing.

This includes everything from organizing the files on your computer, to locking down your social media accounts, to introducing new apps or technologies to make your digital life easier or more secure.

Digital hygiene is a phrase used to refer to the practice of cleaning up your electronic/ information assets and regularly updating them. This process includes knowing how to choose your passwords, organizing files on your laptop, and adjusting the settings on your email and social media accounts, all as part of an effort to ensure greater security. Here are two essential digital hygiene tips to follow.

1.Using Secure Passwords

A strong and unique password can make a significant difference in terms of preventing a future hack (or other cyberattacks). A password is typically considered "strong" if it is long (at least 8 characters) and contains a combination of letters, numbers, and special characters. Many websites will often list a series of requirements and suggestions for strong passwords on their page for creating an account.

2.Protect Computers And Networks From Malware

Malware refers to software that is specifically intended to damage or access a computer network or system without authorization. These types of attacks remain extremely common. According to a 2020 report from Verizon, 28% of data breaches in the first half of 2019 involved malware. Additionally, digital news website CSO recently estimated that 94% of malware is delivered via email.

In order to protect your networks and computers from malware, there are multiple precautions you can take, including:

- *Using antivirus software (which is often free)*
-

Keeping existing software up-to-date

- *Using firewalls*

- *Utilizing pop-up blockers*

Delimitation of the study

The present study is limited to the students of "F.Y.B.Ed" of MES, PCER Chembur.

Methodology of the study

Methodology of the study was a survey type method; google form was made based on the topic "Digital Hygiene". There were 15 number of statements made for google form. They were marked from Agree, Disagree, Strongly Agree and Strongly Disagree, while preparing the research has made the google form based on topic "Digital Hygiene" of research.

Sample of the study

Sample for the study is 17 no. of students of F.Y.B.Ed students of MES, PCER Chembur.

Tool used to collect data

The researcher made a google form consisting of 15 no. of statements with 4 options of answers based on the topic "Digital Hygiene". The google form was first made by the researcher, this was then presented to the research guide for suggestions and modification, after the discussion with the researcher's guide the final tool consisting of 15 questions prepared in the google form. The google form consists of preliminary of the student's respondent.

Selection of tools: The tool used by the researcher to collect the data was a 'questionnaire.'

Questionnaire: A total of 15 statements with 4 standard options were given to collect the relevant information needed for the study.

Preparation of tools: The questionnaire tool consisted of 15 statements in which the students had to choose 1 from the given 4 options. The students had to tick on the option which they felt was most suited to them. These statements were simply framed so that the students could easily understand and tick on the option which suited them.

Analysis of Data

1. *For the research, the google form was sent to the entire class of F.Y.Bed.Thus, The data analysis for the research topic " Digital Hygiene" was done with the help of google form,which consisted of 15 statements in which the students had to choose 1 from the given 4 options. The students had to tick on the option which they felt was most suited to them. These statements were simply framed so that the students could easily understand and tick on the option which suited them. Then the responses from the students were recorded and analysed in the form of pie chart. 1.Maintaining properly functioning devices by protecting them from outside attacks, such as malware, is digital hygiene.*

Interpretation:

94.1% said 'yes' i.e. out of 17 responses 16 has chosen 'yes' and 5.9% i.e., out of 17 responses only 1 response was 'maybe'. It shows that most of the students are aware of digital hygiene. Khan shabeena khatoon taj mohad was was the student for her it might be a new term.

2. Multi-factor authentication is important because a password can be used anywhere, but the other factors like a fingerprint are generally not reproducible by anyone other than you.

Interpretation:

73.5% were agrees to statement i.e., out of 17 responses 13 has chosen 'agree' as their option. 17.6% of students 'strongly agrees' i.e., 3 responses strongly believe factors like fingerprint are generally not reproducible by anyone other than you. However, 5.9% i.e.,1 response 'strongly disagrees' the above statement. The student named Sujoy Mitra has different opinion for the statement.

3.Creating new and unique passwords rooted in passphrases, such as "MyDogIsHappyItsFriday". The longer and more specific the phrase, the less likely a hacker will be able to crack the code.

Interpretation:

The above statement was related to the kind of password that a person should have. Here we can see that 52.9% i.e., out of 17 responses 9 responses 'agrees' to the statement, whereas 23.5% students i.e., 4 responses 'strongly agrees' that longer and more specific the phrase, the less likely the hacker will be able to crack the code. Also we could see that 17.6% students 'disagree' with the statement which means 3 responses and only 5.9% i.e., 1 response was 'strongly disagree' with such password.

4.For maximum security, passwords should be made up of memorable names and dates only.

Interpretation:

47.1%students 'disagree' with the statement which means 8 responses. 29.4% students 'strongly disagree' in keeping memorable names and dates as passwords which is 5 responses. The reason might be that some people are not good in remembering dates or names. But as we can see some students 'agree' in keeping dates and names i.e., 23.5%, 4 responses out of 17.

5.In order to protect your networks and computers from malware, there are multiple precautions such as using antivirus software.

Interpretation:

64.7% students 'agree' that using antivirus software protects your networks and computers from malware, so 11 students responded 'agree'. 6 students 'strongly agree' i.e., 35.3% in order to use antivirus for protecting computers from malware. This shows that most of the students knows that they should not neglect the software protection as it is very important for the system to run smoothly.

6.Identity Theft is due to sharing too much information on social media.

Interpretation:

70.6% students knows that sharing too much information can leads to identity theft, out of 17 responses 12 responses were 'yes'. Whereas, 23.5% students i.e., 4 responses were not sure and selected 'maybe' as their option. Only 1 response given by Aditi Nandkishor Talgaonkar opinion was different, as per her response 'no' I think only sharing information does not create identity theft there might be some other ways which could lead to identity theft.

7.Not responding to security software alerts is an example of security best practices.

Interpretation:

Our computer system shows messages regarding the security software alerts, for the above statement 76.5% of students 'disagree' that not responding to security alerts is security best practices, which means 13 responses. 3 responses i.e., 17.6% 'strongly disagree' for the statement. One student Khan umme Ruman is 'agree' for the statement.

8.Internet security should be looked at as an extension of your personal hygiene.

Interpretation:

Personal hygiene is very important in which we clean and keep things healthy. Likewise internet security is very important. For the above statement 58.8% of students i.e., 10 responses 'agree' that internet security should be looked at as an extension of your personal hygiene. 23.5% of students i.e., 4 responses 'strongly agree' for the above statement, whereas, 17.6% of students which means 3 responses 'disagree' that personal hygiene and internet security is two different things.

9.Organizing your inbox and unsubscribe from junk emails, will reduce the risk of cyberattack.

Interpretation:

Emails, where messages transmitted and received by digital computers through a network, in day-to-day life we receive lots of emails that need to be looked at and be care full from junk emails. Here, 76.5% of students responded 'agree' i.e., 13 students thinks that organizing you inbox and unsubscribe from junk emails, will reduce the risk of cyberattack. Also 23.5% of students 'Strongly agree' with the statement. This shows that students are aware about the emails and organizing the emails.

10.An updated operating system will not only help prevent cyberattacks. It can also lead to enhanced capability, which means that you can carry out many tasks more efficiently.

Interpretation:

Updating system in electronic items like mobile, laptops etc. is important to make them work efficiently. Here 58.8% of students 'agree' that is 10 students think an updated operating system will not only help prevent cyberattacks it can also lead to enhanced capability, which means that you can carry out many tasks more efficiently. 6 responses, 35.3% of students 'strongly agree' to the above statement. However, 1 response given by Hida Peerzade thinks only updating is not enough for enhanced capability.

11.Your personal hotspot is often a safer alternative to free Wi-Fi.

Interpretation:

64.7% of students that is 11 student marked 'yes' for personal hotspot is often a safer alternative to free Wi-Fi. But 35.3% of students, 6 students wasn't sure and marked 'maybe' as their answer.

12.Do you think all the paid conferencing apps are safe for remote learning.

Interpretation:

Remote learning needs to provide study materials for the students, nowadays there are many apps that provide study materials but we need to be care full before we install them. 64.7% of students are not sure and marked 'maybe' as their answer that is 11 students. Whereas, 5 responses i.e., 29.4% of students marked 'no' for the paid conferencing apps for remote learning. Only one response given was 'yes', which means there is a need for awareness among students about the apps.

13.Virus, a malware program that, when executed, replicates by inserting copies of itself (possibly modified) into other computer programs, data files, or firmware.

Interpretation:

Virus, not only affects human life but also in electronic items there are malware such as virus which affects the software of the systems. The analysis shows that 82.4% of students 'agree' which means 14 students responded. 2 students Raveena tripathi and Ankita Singh marked 'disagree' for the statement which is 11.8% of students and only 1 student Sujoy Mitra 'strongly agree' for the above fact related to virus.

14.Malware is made to stop your device from running properly and sometimes to steal your information.

Interpretation:

70.6% of students marked 'true' for the given statement means 12 responses. Some of the students are not sure so they marked 'maybe' that gives 23.5% of students response which means 4 students needs clarification with the concept of malware. Only 1 response given by Khan umme Ruman was marked 'false' and may think malware is not only the reason that could stop or steal information from the system.

15.Separating personal and work stuff whenever possible. Use a dedicated password manager for work, avoid using your personal email for work applications.

Interpretation:

52.9% of students which means 9 students marked 'agree' as their answer and 47.1% of students which means 8 students marked 'strongly agree' for separating personal and work stuff and avoid using personal emails for work applications. This shows that students are very much aware of their personal and work life and knows how to maintain the balance between work and personal life.

Findings:

•

The Best Practices for Digital Hygiene

- *Increase Your Security Methods*
- *Stay Secure With Multiple Passwords*

Suggestions for Teachers

1) Going into online teaching with a learner's mind-set

The success of a new model is dependent largely on how well it is embraced. Moving forward while anticipating teething issues, perhaps such as technological or network issues, and instituting a robust feedback mechanism is crucial. The key is to accept the fact that things may not be as flawless as we would like them to be, despite our best efforts, and meeting challenges with resilience.

2)Prioritize personal connections

Social distancing has been difficult for people of all ages and backgrounds, but especially for kids and teens who rely on their friends for support. Right now, one of the best things you can do is give your students opportunities to make personal connections.

3)Setting the Appropriate Duration

The duration of the online school day should more or less mirror that of a typical school day. Keeping in mind the need to limit screen time, depending on the age of each cohort, only 30 – 40 minutes to a maximum of 3 hours of direct engagement with any device must ideally be prescribed. However, the time the student spends on his/her own on research, inquiry, reflection, practice and written assignments that online classes will enable and support (along with setting time aside for meals, breaks etc), is the key to efficient learning in an online model.

4) Setting Clear Expectations

Traditional face-to-face teaching largely involves instruction and note-taking. However, with the transition to digital devices, it must be acknowledged and accepted that the virtual classroom cannot have the same flow of a traditional one.

The time is upon us to figure out what the new normal is. Moving towards a "blended learning" model – a mix of some real-time interactive online sessions and some offline engagements to reinforce or dive deeper into the concepts – could be a successful approach.

Provide information in multiple ways

In a traditional classroom experience, your students can ask you to explain something or ask for more context. This may not be possible in the e-learning experience. Present information in different ways so that learners with different styles can understand it. Also, make the lesson available in different formats. This could be as simple as downloading a transcript of each lesson. You can also share your PowerPoints, send students additional resources to learn more, and publish your notes to help parents and students study together.Give students as many

Suggestions for Student

- *Use the right tools for digital hygiene*
- *Be thorough, be accurate with digital hygiene*
- *Make digital hygiene part of your routine*
- *Students should Pinpointing specific files for the detection of malicious software.*
- *Scheduling and performing automatic scans.*
- *Scanning either one particular files or your entire computer, or a flash drive, depending on your specific needs.*
- *Erasing malicious codes and software.*
-

Confirming the "health of your computer and other devices.

- *Update software regularly.*
- *Set strong password.*
- *Keep your hard drive clean.*
- *Secure your router*

Conclusion :

Students are aware about the cyber security about some are new to the term digital hygiene. This means we need to work more on the term digital hygiene and make sure that this concept helps the learners to prevent themselves from all kind of malware or thefts as the online working progresses in day-to-day life.

Reference

-

https://www.business-standard.com/article/technology/86-indians-maintain-digital-hygiene-amid-remote-work-says-report-121060200282_1.html

- https://eric.ed.gov/?q=DIGITAL+HYGIENE

- https://www.forbes.com/sites/forbestechcouncil/2020/04/01/hackers-play-dirty-so-practice-good-digital-hygiene/?sh=7f3df6ad3011

- https://hackr.io/blog/what-is-data-analysis-methods-techniques-tools

- https://www.jotform.com/blog/e-learning-experience/

- https://www.livemint.com/

- http://www.math.montana.edu/jobo/phdprep/documents/phd6.pdf

-

https://medium.com/@pubricahealthcare/importance-of-literature-review-in-scientific-research-writing-41d8ea3812c6

- *https://paperpile.com/g/what-is-research-methodology/*

CHAPTER V

"A Study on Impact of Online Learning on Social skills among B.Ed. Students"

Researcher:

Ms. Taifa

Ms. Tanuja Tinu Nadar

S.Y.B.Ed (Batch of 2020-2022), PCER, Chembur

Guided by: *Dr. Reni Francis, Principal, MES's PCER, Chembur*

Abstract: *Generally, it has been seen that children are not very aware of social skills that can be developed in the online classroom. Students are found to isolate themselves from others in the classroom as well as with the* *teacher . In this research paper, the researcher studied the Impact of online learning on social skills among B.ED students. It was found through a graphical data that 25% of the students have developed their social skills in the online spectrum whereas the rest found it difficult. This study was done to create awareness on who to utilize online mode fruitfully. The researcher listed the suggestions for the teachers and the students to bring awareness the same*

Keywords: *Sustainable Developmental Goal, Social Skills*

Introduction to the study

Online learning is the newest and most popular form of distance education today. Within the past decade it has had a major impact on postsecondary education and the trend is only increasing. ***Online education is electronically supported learning that relies on the Internet for teacher/student interaction and the distribution of class materials. Online learning is catalysing a pedagogical shift in how we teach and learn.*** *There is a shift away from top-down lecturing and passive students* *to a more interactive, collaborative approach in which students and instructor cocreate the learning process. The instructor's role is changing from the "sage on the stage" to "the guide on the side."*

BACKGROUND OF THE PROBLEM

Online learning is very different from in-person learning. Students can interact socially with classmates and work together when studying in groups during their learning in the classroom. Meanwhile, when learning online, students only interact with friends or teachers through the help of media with networks. Learning is more often one-way, such as the teacher providing material and assignments, then students working on and collecting them. Some do virtual face-to-face learning using platforms such as zoom or google meets or e-learning built by schools. However, it still has several obstacles, such as a weak network and inadequate facilities.

OBJECTIVES OF THE STUDY

· To study the impact of online learning.

· To study the impact of online learning on social skills.

· To suggest measures for enhancing online learning.

STATEMENT OF PROBLEM

"A Study on Impact of Online Learning on Social skills among B.Ed. Students"

Conceptual definition of the Problem:

*· **Social Skills** – appropriate classroom behaviour, maintaining proper educational attention during instructional periods, non-aversive relationships and interactions with teacher and fellow classmates in school, and non-disruptive classroom behaviour. Whereas, improper or inappropriate social skills is defined where a student fails to exhibit interpersonal social skills that are necessary*

for a student to use as a vehicle to higher aspiration which includes being attentive in class, ability to establish and maintain healthy and friendly relationships with teachers and classmates, and ability to behave in a classroom in a manner that is conducive to learning, The ability to interact with others in ways that will produce positive results – sharing, cooperation, helping.

· ***Online learning***- *A term to describe an emerging approach to learn at students' own premise through advanced information-communication technologies or Learning through the internet via devices that have internet access*

Delimitation of the study

The study is limited to first year B.Ed. students of MES Pillai College of Research and Education.

Methodology of the study

The methodology of the study was Survey type method. The Google form was used to conduct the survey. Google form was made based on the topic "Impact of online learning on Social skills".

There were 15 number of statements made in Google form. The statements were based on the responses i.e., Always, Never, Frequently, Sometimes.

While preparing for the research the researcher has made the google form based on 'impact of online learning on social skills' of research.

Sample of the study

The sample size is a term used in market research for defining the number of subjects included in a sample size. By sample size, we understand a group of subjects that are selected from the general population and is considered a representative of the real population for that specific study. This number is usually represented by n. The size of a sample influences two statistical properties: 1) the precision of our estimates and 2) the power of the study to draw conclusions

For example, if we want to predict how the population in a specific age group will react to a new product, we can first test it on a sample size that is representative of the targeted population. The sample size, in this case, will be given by the number of people in that age group that will be surveyed.

The sample for the study is 18 number of students of first year B.Ed. students from MES Pillai College of Education and Research, Chembur- Mumbai.

Tool used to collect data

Tests are the tools of measurement and it guides the researcher in data collection and also in evaluation. Tools may vary in complexity, interpretation, design and administration. Each tool is suitable for the collection of certain type of information. One has to select from the available tools those which will provide data he seeks for testing hypothesis. It may happen that existing research tools do not suit the purpose in some situation, so researcher should modify them or construct his own. Different tools used for data collection may be-

· *Questionnaires*

· *Interviews*

· *Schedules*

· *Observation Techniques*

· *Rating Scales*

Analysis of Data

The data was analysed in the following using the following steps –

· ***Step 1: Define Your Questions:*** *- The questions were defined understanding that the questions are to either qualify or disqualify potential solutions to the specific problem or* *opportunity.*

· ***Step 2: Set Clear Measurement Priorities: -*** *This step breaks down into two sub steps: A) Decide what to measure, and B) Decide how to measure it.*

· ***Step 3: Collect Data:*** *- The data was collected after the forms were closed for the students of First year B.Ed. students of MES Pillai College of Education and Research.*

· ***Step 4: Analyse Data:*** *- The data was analysed question wise.*

· ***Step 5: Interpretation of Results****: - The data was further interpreted based on observation.*

1. *Online learning helped increasing social skills.*

Interpretations : Almost of the students felt that it was never possible to increase social skills in Online learning but make use of the skills that they already possessed

2.I hesitates to unmute my mike on online platform to avoid everyone's attention on me.

Interpretations: 47.1% of the students said no and 47.1% of students said that they sometimes do this, rest of the students said that they always tend to mute their mikes.

3.I always keep my camera On, while attending online classes.

Interpretations: 66.7% of the students keeps their camera on and 16.7 % of students always keep their camera off.

4. Online learning help me to clear my doubts easily and quickly. Interpretations: Here there was an equal distribution in the answer as 33.3% of students say sometimes, never and always.

5. Online learning made it easy for me to make new friends.

Interpretations: For 50% of students, it was a yes to make new friends sometimes even in the online spectrum.

6.Online learning allows students to share their innovative ideas on various subjects.

Interpretations: 38.9% of students said that it helped sometimes to make new friends online.

7. Online learning lowers the confidence level of the students.

Interpretation: 56.6% of students say that sometimes it made them to lose their confidence

8. Students get freedom of expression on online learning.

Interpretations:33.3% of students feel that it was easy for them to express their feeling always.

9. Students can interact with teachers easily through online learning.

Interpretations: 44.4% of students feel that they frequently got an opportunity to interact with the teacher personally.

10. Student's self-esteem is affected due to online learning.

Interpretations:28.9% of students felt that it was never that they compromised on their self-esteem

11. Online learning have an impact on student's perceptions related to engagement and learning

Interpretations: 16.7% of student always had an impact on their perceptions related to engagement and learning

12. Digital learning materials are more effective in improving social skills of students rather than printed textbooks.

Interpretations:27.8% of students feel that digital learning materials are more effective in improving social skills of students rather than printed textbooks.

13. Self-regulated learning skills is essential for students those who wants to learn in online mode.

Interpretations:38.9% of students felt that Self-regulated learning skills is essential for students those who wants to learn in online mode.

14. Online learning is considered an efficient tool for the development of hard skills such as coding ability, foreign language skills, etc.

Interpretations:55.6% of the students felt that Online learning is considered an efficient tool for the development of hard skills such as coding ability, foreign language skills, etc.

15. Online learning is less effective for improving a student's soft skills i.e. teamwork, problem solving, leadership skills, etc.

Interpretation: 61.1% of the students felt that Online learning is less effective for improving a student's soft skills.

Findings:

Having developed social skills help children to compete with other problem behaviours; they may be prone to have or meet others. It is essential to have a good development of the social skills to have both a positive attitude and to solve the conflicts that may arise – such as externalizing, bullying or hyperactivity.

Social skills help teenagers have better educational and career outcomes, better success in life and create stronger friendships.

Suggestions for Teacher

Inside the school, teachers can promote prosocial behaviour like gratitude, kindness, empathy by:

- *Having a class or some minutes of a class where you practice gratitude by asking students to take some notes on what they feel grateful for.*

- *Encouraging kindness – the more we give compliments and praise, the more students act alike.*

- *Creating a social interaction climate. Whether face to face or online, this is an excellent way for students to develop social skills, as they can see that each person can contribute with something new to the projects. Giving students tasks that mean relying on others to succeed will emphasize social interconnectedness.*

- *Teaching empathy. Empathy must be modelled and taught. The best way to do this is to use personal experiences, as it will help students understand and recognize how other people feel in different situations. Empathy is one of the key characteristics a person with social skills should have.*

- *Helping the students accept and display their emotions. They should understand what each emotion and feeling mean and that they are free to express them.*

Suggestions for Student

- ***Engage with others.*** *Find ways to further conversations with friends, family and close co-workers or practice your conversation skills by asking open-ended questions.*

- ***Greet willingly.*** *Every social interaction begins with greetings. These greetings not only entail phrases such as Hello" or how are you? But also include non-verbal gestures, facial expressions and tone of the voice. In other words, it's not what you say but how you say that lets people know how you truly feel about them. Therefore, students must pay close attention to non-verbal aspects of greeting since they are just as important as spoken words.*

- ***Listen well-*** *In order to maintain and positively engage in a conversation, it is important to listen well and actively. It not only helps you understand the other persons point of view in one go but also eliminates any confusion in conversation. Today, students with relevant social skills would be quick to identify their listener and then frame the response accordingly. Therefore, it is important to not le anything fall on deaf ears.*

- ***Cultivate problem solving abilities-*** *Problems and obstacles are a part-and-parcel of every social interaction. Although it is not the 'difficulties but the 'reaction to these that determines how good are the analytical abilities of a student. So, students should have a positive reaction towards everything as this not only helps in solving problems at a rapid pace but also ensures an atmosphere that is less chaotic. Therefore, students must learn how to turn a conversation from a win-lose" situation to* *a win-win" situation in order to effectively resolve conflicts.*

- **Apologise, whenever required**- *It is human to err, therefore, one must accept whenever we make mistakes and commit blunders. Apologising is a courageous act and helps in swiftly correct one's own mistakes. This helps the student to grow individually, both in personal and school/professional lives. At present times, apologising is the most important social skill as it elevates acceptance among peers.*

Conclusion

The best way to develop your child's social skills is just like every other skill. Practice! You'll need to make sure they have kids to play with to practice those skills. If you live in a neighbourhood with a lot of kids, you are lucky! Neighbourhood kids are a great place to start, but if you don't have a lot of options around you head for the park, the pool, invite friends from school over or take them with you on some family activities. Siblings, while they tend to fight the very most, are another excellent source of social skill building.

References

· *Books*

· *Action Research : Researches on Classroom Problem by MES's Pillai College of Education and Research, Chembur.*

· *Website links :*

files.eric.ed.gov/fultext/ED529283.pdf

- https://hbsp.harvard.edu/inspiring-minds/online-learning-can-still-be-social

- https://spark.school/wellbeing/student-wellbeing/the-importance-of-social-skills-

in-early-education

- *https://stanfield.com/7-strategies-help-students-develop-social-skills-summer-break/*

- *https://tophat.com/glossary/o/online-learning/*

- *https://uscupstate.libguides.com/c.php?g=627058&p=4389968*

- *https://www.ascilite.org/conferences/brisbane99/papers/lynch.pdf*

- *https://www.niu.edu/citl/resources/guides/increase-student-engagement-in-online-courses.shtml*

- *https://www.readingrockets.org/article/9-ways-teach-social-skills-your-classroom*

- *https://www.scribbr.com/dissertation/literature-review/*

-

journals.plos.org/plosone/article?id=10.1371/journal.pone.0250378

- *https://er.educause.edu/articles/2007/2/how-students-develop-online-learning-skills*

- *https://www.frontiersin.org/articles/10.3389/feduc.2021.705013/full*

CHAPTER VI

"A Study of Impact of Online learning on Technological adaptability among the B.Ed. students"

Researcher: Ms.Vairavalakshmi Chelliah

S.Y.B.Ed. (Batch of 2020-2022), PCER, Chembur

Guided by: Dr.Reni Francis, Principal, MES's PCER, Chembur

Abstract:

No one imagines that Covid-19 would turn our world upside down and would bring major changes to our life style. Online classes and technology have emerged as a superhero during the lockdown days. Adopting to advanced technology was at ease but adapting to them requires skills, practice and patience. In this research paper the researcher studied the impact of technological adaptability in online learning among the B.Ed. students of PCER,

Chembur. It was found that 43.8% of the students responded that getting adapted to new technologies did reinforce their online learning but also many-faced trouble adapting to new technologies. This study was done to understand the effect of using new technologies in online learning. The researcher listed the suggestions for teachers and students to develop the ability to adapt new technical skills in online learning.

Keywords: Technological adaptability, Online learning

Introduction to the study

The education that takes place online or over the internet is called online learning. Another name for online learning is e-learning. It is the type of education that requires computers, laptops or smartphones and a high-speed internet connection. Online learning is also used in schools and colleges. This method is beneficial in cases where students are living in a remote location. A lot of institutions worldwide offer online to students who do not have access to a physical classroom. Online learning offers a wide range of options for students. Students can decide the course as per their area of interest. The said type of learning has multifaceted benefits. It gives ease of learning for students; Individuals can also reschedule the class if they miss it for any reason. Online teaching has a lot of advantages and a lot of teachers have shifted to teaching online. Working professionals who do not have time to attend a class physically prefer learning online.

Background of the problem

In the traditional classroom students were taught using materials that are readily in the remote areas. When there is a rise in use of online learning it becomes essential for students to learn and acquire technical skills. During the pandemic, education system was forced to shift online, it became necessary for all to learn and teach online. Many faced obstacles understanding and adapting the new system, it became a necessity to learn new skills to make the learning effective and engaging, this research studies how students get affected while accessing online education using technology

Objectives of the study

1.To study the impact of online learning

2.To study the impact of technological adaptability in online learning 3.To suggest measures for enhancing online learning

Statement of the problem

"A Study of Impact of Online learning on Technological adaptability among B.Ed. Students"

Conceptual definition of the problem

Study:

Conceptual definition: *It is the act of learning and spending time discovering information or an academic work or investigation about a particular thing or subject area.*

Operational definition: *To find the impact of online learning on technological adaptability among students.*

Technological Adaptability:

Conceptual definition*: an ability to deal with the technology changes, learn new-age skills, and work with a number of technocrats who are working on a wide spectrum of technology.*

Operational definition: *an ability to move quickly and adapt to changes in customer demands, technology advancements and disruptive competition better than those rely on size and efficiency alone.*

Online learning:

Conceptual definition*: Education that takes place over the internet. It is often referred to as 'e-learning'.*

Operational definition: *Web based learning allows instructors to deliver the same content using different media, like videos or simulations, personalizing learning.*

B.Ed. students:

Conceptual definition: *Students pursuing B.Ed. of Pillai College of Education and Research*

Operational definition: *Students pursuing B.Ed. of Pillai College of Education and Research*

Delimitations of the study

The study is delimited to;

The students of Pillai College of Education and Research

Students of F.Y.B.Ed. only.

Students studying in English Medium College

Methodology of the study

Research methodology is defined as a highly intellectual human activity used in the investigation of nature and matter and deals specifically with the manner in which data is collected, analysed and interpreted system of models, procedures and techniques used to find the result of a research problem is called research methodology

Sample of the study

The sample for the study is 16 students of F.Y.B.Ed. students MES PCER, Chembur ***Tool used to collect data***

The researcher made a google form consisting of 15 statements with 5 options of answers based on "A study of Impact of Online learning on Technological adaptability". The google form was first made by the researcher this was then presented to the research guide for suggestions and modifications. After the discussion with the research guide the final tool consisting of 15 questions was prepared as a google form. The google form consisted of preliminary information of a student respondent

Analysis of Data

The research reflects on the effects of online learning on technological adaptability. During the Covid-19 outbreak it was difficult and impossible to study and learn in an offline environment, in order to tackle this issue, the education shifted to online mode wherein the learner can learn from his/her own environment. There seems to be rise in use of new technologies to promote distance learning ,online courses, seminars, webinars and many more. Adopting this advanced technology was at ease but adapting to these technologies is a challenge and that requires skills, practice, patience and acceptance. The sudden change does affect the learners in various ways and this research helps us to study the impact of online learning on technological adaptability. The research collected 16 responses from the respondents who are the first-year students pursuing Bachelors of Education from PCER, Chembur. The researcher used google form to collect responses.

In order to find the impact of online learning on technological adaptability, the following questions asked were:

1.In online learning, getting adapted to new technologies by students directly affects the student's effectiveness of online learning.

Interpretation:

We could say that about 43.8% i.e., 7 respondents agree to the statement and 31.3% i.e., 5 respondents stay neutral to the statement and the rest of the 25% i.e., 4 respondents strongly agree to the statement

2.There is no significant difference in the student perception towards latest technology across the age

Interpretation:

we can say that almost 43.8% i.e. 7 respondents agree to the statement given above,25% 4 responses were neutral other 25% i.e., 4 respondents agree to the statement and 6.3% i.e., 1 strongly disagree to the question.

3.Did u face any problem while getting adapted to new technologies

Interpretation:

About 81.3% i.e., 13 of the respondents said No to the statement and 12.5% i.e., 2 respondents said Yes to the statement and the remaining 6.3% i.e., 1 responded May be to the statement

4.In online learning, adaptation of new technologies enables students to deepen their understanding of difficult concepts

Interpretation:

50% of the responses that is nearly 8 respondents agree to the statement and 25% of the responses that is 4 respondents remains neutral ,18.8% of the responses that is 3 respondents strongly agree to the statement and the remaining 1 respondent occupying 6.3% of the chart disagrees to the statement.

5.Technological adaptation provides students with easy to access information, accelerated learning and fun opportunities

Interpretation:

56.3% respondents that is 9 of them agreed to the statement,31.3% of the respondents that is 5 of them strongly agreed to the statements,12.5% of the respondents that is 2 of them have responded neutral

6.Has technological adaptations helped keep engagement in virtual classrooms high

Interpretation:

37.5% that is 6 respondents remained neutral to the statement ,37.5% that is 6 respondents have agreed to the statements and the remaining 4 respondents occupying 25% of the chart strongly agreed to the statement.

7.Technological adaptations in online learning has opposed to the past tradition of one-sided conversation

Interpretation:

Around 7 respondents that is 43.8% of them have responded neutral to the statement,4 respondents that is 25% of the responses received have agreed to the statement,3 of them have disagreed to the statement and 2 of them have strongly agreed to the statement.

8.With Technical adaptations learning is becoming more feasible day by day

Interpretation:

Among the 16 respondents 11 of them comprising 68.8% of the pie chart have responded Yes to the statement,4 respondents that is 25% of them have responded May be to the statement and the remaining 1 respondent of 6.3% have responded No to the statement

9.We must have the knowledge of basic technologies to handle the forth coming or advanced adaptations in technology

Interpretation:

87.5% of the respondents which is 14 respondents have responded Yes to the statement, remaining 12.5% i.e., 2 respondents responded May be to the statement

10.Can each and every student in the classroom easily adapt to the technology changes during online learning.

Interpretation:

About 37.5% i.e., over 6 respondents have responded neutral to the statement ,31.3% I.e., 5 of them have agreed to the statement ,4 respondents have disagreed to the statement and 1 respondent strongly disagreed to the statement.

11.My ability to retain information has reduced due to online learning.

Interpretation:

6 respondents i.e., 37.5% have agreed to the statement whereas other 6 i.e., 37.5% have disagreed to the statement.3 respondents i.e.,18.8% have responded neutral and one strongly disagrees to the statement

12.Over dependence on technology has led to students losing their creativity, ability to think.

<u>Interpretation:</u>

31.3% that is 5 of them have responded neutral ,25% that is 4 of the respondents agrees and 4 disagrees to the statement remaining 12.5% i.e., 2 strongly agrees to the statement and 1 strongly disagrees to the statement

13.Every school is capable of adopting new technological products <u>Interpretation:</u>

31.3% that is 5 respondents have disagreed to the statement,37.5% that is 6 of them have agreed to the statement and 18.8% that is 3 respondents remained neutral to the statement and the remaining 12.5% that is 2 have strongly agreed to the statement

14.Maintaining ethics during online lectures and online exams have reduced.

<u>Interpretation:</u>

43.8% i.e., 7 respondents have responded neutral to the statement 37.5% of the respondents comprising 6 respondents have agreed to the statement.1 respondent strongly disagrees,1 respondent disagrees and 1 respondent strongly agrees to the statement.

15.Adopting new technological products will make it easier for future educators to assess students

Interpretation:

43.8% that is 7 respondents have strongly agreed to the statement 37.5% i.e., 6 respondents have agreed to the statement and the remaining 3 respondents responded neutral to the statement

Findings

Technological adaptability is a skill which is much needed to learn through online Accessing to new technologies helps us to enhance our knowledge Technological adaptability widens the ability to adapt to any challenging circumstances an individual being put through

It also makes the learning personalised, effective and fun.

Its normal to be confused or baffled when initially introduced to a new system, but when we start to use in regular basis, we get adapted to it

Suggestions for Teacher

- *Training to learn basic and advanced technical skills need to be provided for teachers. Updating themselves to the current technological products to incorporate in day-to-day teaching.*
-

Learning AI courses to gain knowledge which shall be used in virtual learning. Attending workshops online would enhance their teaching level.

•

Trying and exploring varied technological products.

•

Seeking assistance from colleagues to know how they use technical learning in online. Taking hybrid class mode in case of crisis.

•

Connect to students individually and knowing their needs.

•

"Consistency is the key" learning and updating regularly is a must. Making a reflective journal of the daily happenings.

•

Searching and using right resources.

•

Suggestion for Students:

•

Attending seminar and workshops

•

Communicating with the teachers

- *Using varied resources to learn about technological products*

- *Additional courses to learn about AI and coding*

- *Attending regular sessions to be consistent*

- *Self-learning is must*

- *Taking a time out*

Conclusion

Adapting to new technology helps us to be ready whenever the circumstances changes eg,Covid-19 crisis. When learning through online new technology helps us to make the learning more efficient, effective, engaging and flexible. Online learning is user friendly but the side effects of using it for a long period does affect the cognitive domain and make the person over dependent on it. Maintaining ethics during online lectures and exams is seem to be questionable and its normal for a human being to be confused when introduced to a new system but when there is continuity of the learning any individual can adapt to the technologies.

References

eric.ed.gov

https://libguides.unf.edu/litreview/benefits

https://www.lighthouselabs.ca/en/blog/the-five-stages-of-data analysis

www.researchgate.net

www.simplilearn.com

theimportantsite.com

https://www.voxco.com/blog/what-is-research/

https://www.ey.com/en_us/innovation/the-importance-of adaptability-in-an-increasingly-complex-world

Concluding Note

The research presented in this publication is a part of the Action Research conducted by student teachers as a part of the B.Ed curriculum for the academic year 2020-2022.

Printed by Libri Plureos GmbH in Hamburg, Germany